The
Disappointment
Dragon

The
Disappointment Dragon

Learning to cope with disappointment (for all children and dragon tamers, including those with Asperger syndrome)

K.I. Al-Ghani

Illustrations by Haitham Al-Ghani

Jessica Kingsley *Publishers*
London and Philadelphia

First published in 2014
by Jessica Kingsley Publishers
73 Collier Street
London N1 9BE, UK
and
400 Market Street, Suite 400
Philadelphia, PA 19106, USA

www.jkp.com

Library of Congress Cataloging in Publication Data
Al-Ghani, K. I.
  The disappointment dragon : learning to cope with disappointment (for all children and dragon tamers,
including those with Asperger syndrome) / K.I. Al-Ghani ; illustrated by Haitham Al-Ghani.
    pages cm
  ISBN 978-1-84905-432-4 (alk. paper)
 1. Disappointment in children--Juvenile literature. 2. Adjustment (Psychology) in children--Juvenile
literature. I. Al-Ghani, Haitham, illustrator. II. Title.
  BF723.D47A42 2014
  155.4'124--dc23
                          2013030791

British Library Cataloguing in Publication Data
A CIP catalogue record for this book is available from the British Library

ISBN 978 1 84905 432 4
eISBN 978 0 85700 780 3

Printed and bound in China

This book is dedicated to Ahmed and Sarah Al-Ghani, for their continued support and encouragement, and to my mother, Elizabeth, who is Haitham's biggest fan.

Contents

Introduction

Disappointment happens when things don't turn out the way we want or expect. It is an unfortunate aspect of living, and yet most of us are guilty of wanting to shield our children from life's disappointments. It seems we are emotionally programmed to want children to be carefree, to live a life filled with positive experiences and happy expectations. However, by trying to create a life free from disappointment and failure, we may inadvertently be doing them a disservice. We should instead be helping children to overcome life's hardships by resisting the temptation to rescue them from failure and by teaching them how to cope when the "Disappointment Dragon" comes to visit.

Typical children learn to read adult reactions to challenging situations and then use this knowledge as a sort of guide to learn how they should react to their own disappointments, frustrations and failures. If you have ever watched one of those fly-on-the-wall airport programmes, you can observe the reactions of disappointed adults when they have just missed their flight. Those picked to feature on these programmes are the ones who react very badly. Some become openly confrontational with the airport staff, others emit a string of expletives, and some dissolve into floods of tears.

If we are to help children to cope with life, then we have to learn to react to disappointment stoically, from a position of acceptance and faith, rather than fear or anger. We must show children, by example, that our response to difficulties and disappointment is tempered with a sense of perspective. When children look to us for help and comfort, we must learn to shield them from our own anxiety by showing them a measured perspective and a calm acceptance of the situation.

This approach is especially important for children with Asperger syndrome (AS). We need to be careful that these children do not blame us when plans go awry or hopes are crushed. Their black-and-white thinking and difficulty understanding the perspective of others can sometimes lead to persistent negative thoughts and attributions of blame, especially if a situation which has resulted in disappointment is not adequately understood and subsequently resolved. We should also be more understanding, since emotional maturity for the child with AS is often two or three years behind that of a typical child. Many children, especially those with AS, learn to develop a standard response to everything, irrespective of scale. They often resort to screaming, crying, tantrums or sulking.

We know that brains and minds are shaped by experience. This plasticity makes it possible for us to continue to learn throughout our life and so it is never too late to change! All children should learn to distinguish between the serious and the trivial. While not trivialising their disappointments, we need to teach them how to take a measure of perspective. Is the problem something that can be repaired or replaced? Can it be postponed or managed without? We can listen to children and let them see that we will help them towards a resolution, but ultimately they must learn to decide how they will choose to respond and consequently banish that Disappointment Dragon. We must teach realistic hope, based on a fair estimation of probability. We can teach children simple strategies to use, so they will know what to do to save themselves (and others) from embarrassment and needless heartache.

Research has shown that people cannot survive without hope. Hope is a very important motivational tool. Hope keeps negative emotions at bay and with it we learn to live our lives with positive potential. The opposite of hope is despair; a very dark and gloomy place. It is the place we are taken by the Disappointment Dragon and we must help children to banish this dragon, so that they can recover and find the "Dragon of Hope". It is possible to train children to choose hope over despair. As children learn how to do this, we can then display genuine pride when they handle disappointments in a mature way.

It is my hope that the stories of the Disappointment Dragon will highlight some common childhood frustrations and open the door to discussion with children about their own battles with disappointment.

At the end of the book you will find a list of suggestions and strategies for dealing with disappointment. By using some of these, I hope every child will learn how to banish the Disappointment Dragon and transfer those negative emotions to the Dragon of Hope.

Note: Care should be taken if normal disappointment seems to result in long-term depression. This may then point to a more serious mental health issue and the child should be referred to a specialist practitioner.

The Disappointment Dragon

This is the Disappointment Dragon.

Everybody knows him and nobody likes him.

He shows up when we have had our hopes
dashed and our dreams destroyed.

The Disappointment Dragon would like us to choose to travel
with him to his home in the Valley of Despair. He would
like us to stay with him there for as long as possible. You
see, our disappointments fuel his flight, and, if we let him,
he can fly us deep into his valley of sadness and regrets.

You have probably heard this before and I am
sure you will hear it again: LIFE ISN'T FAIR.

We don't always get what we need or what we deserve, and
so everyone must learn how to manage the Disappointment
Dragon. If we choose to let him take control of our emotions,
he can make us feel sad and miserable for a very long time.

The Disappointment Dragon loves children. He knows that
little ones just don't know how to cope when things don't
go their way. When disappointment strikes, they scream
and rage and stamp their feet! This fills the Disappointment
Dragon with glee and sometimes he is able to get his
fiery breath blowing, just like in the olden days!

Grown-ups have ways to help little children banish the Disappointment Dragon. They can hold them tight, rock them in the rocking chair, sing soothing songs and give them a back rub. Before too long, they have helped the child to leave the Disappointment Dragon and the Valley of Despair and move to the Mountain of Happiness, where the sun shines warm and bright again. Here they can find the Dragon of Hope.

The Disappointment Dragon just cannot compete with the Dragon of Hope and so he flies off to his valley to wait for his next chance to swoop.

As children grow older, however, they are expected to learn how to deal with the Disappointment Dragon on their own, especially when other people are around. Having a temper tantrum is just not right! The Disappointment Dragon can make us act in an embarrassing way in front of strangers, teachers, school friends and relatives.

This book can give you some ideas that will help you to learn how to banish the Disappointment Dragon and find your way to the Dragon of Hope's Mountain of Happiness.

In the following stories we will see how the Disappointment Dragon creeps up on some of the children in Class 3 of Churchill Primary School.

The Disappointment Dragon and Making the Team

This is Bobby Fisher.

Bobby has been practising his football skills all month. Grandpa couldn't help noticing how seriously Bobby had been taking this training, so he asked him about it.

"I'm hoping to get picked for the school football team, Grandpa," Bobby told him excitedly.

"That's good, Bobby," replied Grandpa, "but aren't you too young to be chosen for the team?"

"Maybe," said Bobby, "but if I am good, they are sure to pick me," he boasted.

"Well," said Grandpa wisely, "sometimes things don't always go to plan. I think you should prepare yourself, just in case you *don't* make the team. Do you know, Bobby, when I was about your age, *I* didn't get picked for the school team. I was so disappointed that I did something really embarrassing."

"Just like you," he went on, "I was sure I'd get picked. When my name wasn't read out, I rushed over to the coach and shouted at him. The coach and the other kids all looked shocked. Instead of sympathising with me, they called me a big baby. I was so mad that I kicked over a bottle of orange juice and tried to hit one of the boys. I got into real trouble, I can tell you. It was then that the Disappointment Dragon turned up and I got a free ride way down to the Valley of Despair!"

Bobby's eyes grew wide.

"What happened then, Grandpa?" Bobby asked curiously.

"When my dad heard what had happened, he was really angry. He said it was time I learned to pull myself together and stop being such a cry baby!"

"Yeah," Bobby said, rolling his eyes, "people say that to me all the time and it makes me even angrier!"

"Well, do you know," Grandpa said, with a wink, "I didn't realise it was just an expression and so I really would 'pull myself together'. When I felt disappointed, I would quickly sit down, cross my arms over my chest and grab my arms. Then I would do a slow countdown from ten to zero. It never failed and it certainly stopped me from hitting and kicking *and* it stopped the Disappointment Dragon from taking me too deep into the Valley of Despair."

Bobby was amazed. He had never thought of disappointment as a dragon before.

"What did you do then, Grandpa?" asked Bobby eagerly.

"Well, if I was upset because I had lost a game or wasn't picked for a team, my dad told me to copy the behaviour of the winners. I still felt sad, but when I saw the winners smiling and patting each other on the back, I would get up and try to do that. People would be really nice to me and pretty soon I felt much better," explained Grandpa encouragingly.

For the rest of the week Bobby and Grandpa practised "pulling themselves together". They made a sliding scale from one to ten to show how likely it was that Bobby would get picked for the team, and Bobby saw that there was only a slight chance he would get picked because of his age.

On the day of the tryouts, sadly, Bobby didn't get picked for the team. However, he did put Grandpa's plan into action. He sat down on the bench and, taking a deep breath, he "pulled himself together". Then he got up and congratulated the kids that had been chosen.

The coach noticed Bobby's reaction so he had a word with him as the others were leaving. "Well done, Bobby," he said proudly, "I like the way you handled that disappointment. I shall be putting you to the top of the list for the next tryouts."

The coach also spoke to Bobby's mum and she was so proud of him. Needless to say, when Grandpa heard all about it, he smiled broadly, crossed his arms over his chest and winked at Bobby.

You'll be pleased to know that Bobby did get on the school team the following year.

The Disappointment Dragon and the Chicken Pox

Class 3 of Churchill Primary School were very excited. On Friday they would all be going on a school trip to the Sea Life Centre with Miss Robertson, their class teacher.

However, the day before the trip, little Lucinda Formby wasn't feeling so good. She felt hot and itchy and that night, as she got ready for bed, Mum noticed a rash on her body. It was chicken pox.

Of course, this meant Lucinda wouldn't be able to go on the school trip. She begged Mum to let her go, but Mum explained that she would be in quarantine for a week. This meant she was to stay at home so the other children would not catch the chicken pox from her.

Lucinda was very disappointed and she cried herself to sleep that night.

The next morning, Lucinda was with the Disappointment Dragon way down in the Valley of Despair. When Mum came in with the breakfast tray she hid under the bedclothes and refused to come out.

"Now, Lucinda," said Mum coaxingly, "I know that you are very disappointed about missing the trip, but Granny has promised to take you as soon as you are better."

"I don't want to go with Granny," shouted Lucinda, ungratefully, from under the quilt.

"Do you know, when I was a little girl," Mum went on, changing the subject, "your Granny used to give me the 'Distraction Box' when I was ill in bed. I am sure I still have it somewhere. I'll give you a few minutes to think about things and then I'll bring the box in when you are feeling a little brighter."

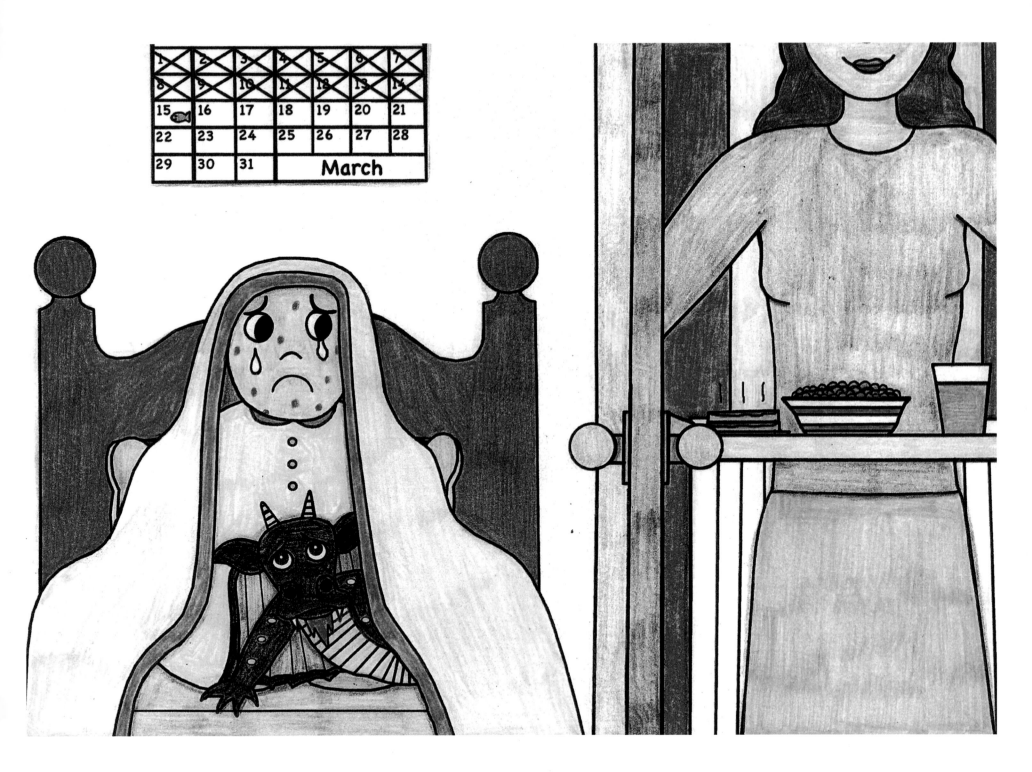

As soon as Mum had left the room, Lucinda came out from under the covers. At first her thoughts were all about school and how the children would be getting on the bus now. It made her feel very miserable and the Disappointment Dragon was rather pleased.

However, whispering in her ear was the Dragon of Hope. He reminded Lucinda about the Distraction Box. Thinking about this box helped Lucinda to leave the Valley of Despair and find her way to the Mountain of Happiness.

The Disappointment Dragon hated it here, it was far too warm and bright and cheerful. The hope shining from this place hurt his eyes and he had no choice but to fly back down to his gloomy home, alone.

By the time Mum came back, Lucinda had eaten a little breakfast and was sitting up in bed wondering what would be in the box.

The Distraction Box was an old hat box decorated with flowers cut from colourful wrapping paper.

Mum explained that when she was a child, if Granny found an interesting object she would wrap it in tissue paper and put it in the box. If any of the children were ill, they were allowed to play with the contents of the box.

Lucinda couldn't wait to look inside. She carefully lifted the lid and saw many items wrapped in brightly coloured tissue paper. She felt very excited at the thought of unwrapping each little parcel.

At this point, the Disappointment Dragon knew he had lost out to the Dragon of Hope and so he didn't have the strength to fly Lucinda back down to the Valley of Despair again that day.

In the box, Lucinda found lots of interesting things, including a little mirror and lip gloss, a tiny pen and notebook, and a kaleidoscope that showed many beautiful patterns as you turned it. There was a little doll with extra clothes for dressing up, a miniature teddy bear, some smooth stones, a little book of baby animals, and many more exciting objects.

The morning just flew by without thoughts of school and soon it was time for lunch and a nap. Lucinda was still sorry to have missed the trip, but the box had helped her to forget her sadness.

When she was well again, Mum hid the box away.

Lucinda often played Distraction Box with her dolls. Whenever she could, she would put something in an old shoe box for the game.

When Lucinda returned to school, Miss Robertson gave her a blue whale key ring she had bought from the Sea Life Centre. I think you can guess where Lucinda put it, can't you?

The Disappointment Dragon and Goodbye Miss Robertson

One Monday morning, near the end of the school year, the children in Class 3 of Churchill Primary School were met by a most unusual sight. Miss Robertson, their class teacher, was sitting at her desk with a large box over her head. The box had been made to look just like a television set and there was a notice on her desk saying:

"PLEASE SIT IN YOUR MORNING SPACE AND WAIT QUIETLY FOR AN IMPORTANT NEWS BULLETIN."

The children grinned at each other as they quickly sat in the morning circle with their arms folded and a finger pressed firmly on their lips, eyes shining with eager anticipation.

Miss Robertson was an extraordinary teacher, she made every school day seem special. On the door to her room was a notice that read:

"THE ONLY DISABILITY IN LIFE IS A BAD ATTITUDE. DON'T BRING ONE INTO THIS ROOM. THANK YOU!"

When the children were settled, Miss Robertson pointed to the register. Today it was Lucinda Formby's turn to read out the names, so she went to sit on the helper's high chair. After calling the register, she asked the children to put their hand up if they wanted a school dinner so she could record the number.

When those little jobs were done, Lucinda signalled for the class to start chanting the eight times table, while she took the lists along to the school office. She got back just as they were finishing.

When Lucinda returned to the circle, Miss Robertson turned the knob on the "television" and announced:

> *"Good morning. Today we have some breaking news. Miss Robertson of Churchill Primary School is to be married to Mr Timothy Burgess. The wedding will take place on the 20th July, 2013, at her local church."*

All the children clapped and cheered.

Miss Robertson waited patiently for the children to settle down again and then she continued with the news bulletin.

"Soon after the wedding, Mr and Mrs Burgess will be emigrating to New Zealand to start a new life together."

There was a collective gasp as all the children struggled to understand what she had just said. An eerie hush fell over the classroom and suddenly Lucinda burst into tears.

Miss Robertson was astonished. She had felt sure the children would be as excited as she was about her news. Quietly, she removed the box and, putting an arm around Lucinda, she explained that all this would be happening at the end of the school year and so it would not really affect them since they would all be moving up to a new class.

The children had been trying not to think about this. They all wished they could stay in Class 3 for ever.

At lunch that day one of the boys, Nigel Collins, came up with a brilliant suggestion. "I think, instead of feeling sad, we should think up some ways to thank Miss Robertson and wish her a happy life," he said wisely.

Thinking about doing something nice for Miss Robertson made the children forget about their sadness and the Disappointment Dragon lost his hold on them. The children decided that they would each write and illustrate a letter to Miss Robertson, describing a lesson they had particularly enjoyed.

Lucinda loved the lesson they did about travel, where they had each made a passport and then pretended they were on an aeroplane.

Bobby Fisher enjoyed the lesson they did on Goliath. The children had made a life-sized drawing of Goliath and then took turns, using a sling, to hurl baby tomatoes and marshmallows at the giant.

There was no shortage of ideas.

On the last day of term, the children presented their letters to Miss Robertson in a special folder with a bag that she could use on her journey. Miss Robertson was so delighted!

"Do you know, children, this is the best present I have ever received. I shall cherish it and remember each and every one of you when I look at it," she said, holding back the tears.

The children had even sent copies of the letters to the head teacher, who was going to publish them in the school magazine.

The children of Class 3 Churchill Primary School had all chosen to look for the Dragon of Hope as they looked forward to the long summer holidays and the chance of another excellent teacher when they returned to school in the autumn.

How to Banish the Disappointment Dragon

Disappointment affects children in different ways, but most of them usually end up pouting, shouting or clouting.

For children whose disappointment turns quickly to anger, they may end up shouting and screaming or hitting out at people or objects. To overcome their disappointment these children will need to learn how to keep their bodies under control. For children who are more restrained, disappointment may lead to "pouting", which manifests itself as crying, sulking or grumbling.

Here are some ways to help children to banish the Disappointment Dragon:

"Get a grip" and "Pull yourself together"

- 🐾 To stem violence and destruction to property you must first get the children to sit down. This will stop movement and the possibility of kicking. Next they should fold their arms over their chest and grab their upper arms. The children must then breathe in deeply and count down from ten to zero.

- 🐾 Some children with AS do not like to cross over the mid-line with their arms. Train them to sit on their hands or put their hands in their pockets, then do the countdown pushing down into the floor or chair.

"Suck it up!"

🐾 To help prevent children shouting, swearing or saying something they may later regret, they need to learn to "suck it up". Let them imagine they are sucking up some extra-thick milkshake. Suck up to a count of ten and then let the breath out slowly. They can practise this when calm using a straw and a grape. Ask them to suck up the grape and see how long they can hold it before dropping it. Focus on breathing in the calm and blowing out, using bubbles or feathers to help them to visualise this.

🐾 Replace swear words with a more acceptable response, for example, Sugar! Bother! Fudge! Shoot! Blast! Cheese and crackers! Holey socks and shoes! Monkey doos! Fiddlesticks! No, no, my big toe! Oh, grasshoppers! Have fun making these up.

"Take a hike"

🐾 If possible, let the children go for a brisk walk. If in school, children could pace the corridors counting to 100 steps before returning to class, or jog round the perimeter of the school playground.

🐾 Children with AS could have a "get out" card that they can show when they need to take some time out. You will need to practise using this card when the child is calm, so that they will know how to use it when they are angry.

🐾 Younger children could learn to jog on the spot while counting to 100 and then shake out their hands and feet vigorously. As they do this they could say a little rhyme (see the examples below).

Make up a mantra

List life's little disappointments and make up a rhyme. For example:

I lost the game
Must not complain
Shake! Shake! Shake!

Missed the bus
Don't make a fuss
Shake! Shake! Shake!

Burnt the cake
For goodness sake
Shake! Shake! Shake!

Failed the test
Such a pest
Shake! Shake! Shake!

Distract the Dragon

- Look at a "Happy Scrap Book" – compiled by the child and filled with images that make them smile.

- Go to look at an aquarium – many schools have these. Better still, think of having one at home – super soothing.

- Listen to some uplifting or soothing music on an iPod – sing or dance along.

- Prepare a "Distraction Box" – collect interesting or nostalgic items.

- Help to develop a passion for something – stamp collecting, Lego, coins, needlepoint, knitting, pottery, a musical instrument…

Get cosy

- Take a hot, bubbly bath and soak away the cares.

- Roll yourself up in a sweet-smelling quilt.

- Ask for a hug.

- Have a refreshing drink of water, through a straw.

- Suck on a popsicle.

- Go to the rocking chair or swing.

Note: Be careful about comfort eating. Associating disappointment with eating can lead to obesity – it is true that chocolate and cheesecake can be exceedingly comforting, but we should not be encouraging children to make this association.

"Laugh it off"

- Read a comic book or watch some old-fashioned cartoons.
- Have a box of funny films and choose one to watch.
- Watch an episode of Mr Bean, Laurel and Hardy or the Marx Brothers on YouTube.
- Try to find the funny side of the problem.

Talk to the Dragons

- Encourage the children to acknowledge their feelings and then say something like:

  "Okay, I know I am here in your valley, but I am not staying long."

  "I feel really upset, but I am not going with you. I can sit and think what to do."

  "You can't keep me in this valley, life has other things to offer."

  "Hey, Dragon of Hope, get me out of here!"

- Use a mantra:

  I am disappointed

  But I won't play

  Disappointment Dragon – GO AWAY!

  I am feeling low

  But I don't want to go

  To the Valley of Despair – No! No! No!

Banish the Dragon with creativity

- Draw or paint a picture.

- Do a puzzle.

- Bake some biscuits or cupcakes.

- Write a letter or a story.

- Make a model.

- Press flowers.

- Do brass rubbing.

- Plan and cook supper for the family.

- Pitch a tent.

- Do some dressing up.

- Go bargain hunting in your local charity shop.

- Plant some flowers or vegetables.

Note: Be careful using computer games – these often lead to tension and can result in more disappointment if the computer crashes or the child fails to make the next stage.

Develop a sense of perspective

On a scale of one to ten, decide how big the problem is. List possible disappointments and put them on this scale.

Discuss ways of dealing with them in a mature way. For example, "We can't have a dog, but we could get a hamster, fish, turtle…"

True success is not all about getting your own way. It is about finding alternatives.

"Be prepared"

Work out the probability of something going wrong. Make a sliding scale, with a moving arrow going from Impossible to Highly Likely. Now make a list of events and slide the arrow to work out the probability. For example:

- Winning the lottery.

- Walking on the moon.

- Watching the sunset tomorrow.

- Winning the class prize for History.

- Getting picked for the football team.

- Scoring a goal.

- Getting a new mobile (cell) phone.

- Having a sleepover.

- Getting a puppy.

A final note to parents and carers

When dealing with childhood disappointment, take on the role of sage and confidante. Listen to the children, but resist the temptation to "fix" the situation.

Always give time to allow the crisis point to pass. Let them know you are ready to help when they want you, even if it is only to give a reassuring hug. Let the children go to a place where they can cry if they wish, and where they can take time to think about the situation. Crying is very cathartic; it involves hormones that calm the body.

Be supportive and try not to get emotional yourself.

Familiarise the children with the strategies above and give them plenty of opportunities to practise different scenarios when they are calm and in control. Link these scenarios to a calm feeling. Occasionally, turn the tables. Let them know when you are disappointed and ask their advice.

Always praise children when they resolve a situation themselves and show pride when they demonstrate emotional maturity. In this way you will raise well-balanced children who will be able to face whatever life throws at them. They will learn that they have the power to choose hope instead of despair.